AF599110

Pioneers of Space

by Alex Hall

Minneapolis, Minnesota

Credits
Images are courtesy of Shutterstock.com. With thanks to Getty Images, Thinkstock Photo, and iStockphoto. Recurring images – Elena Pimukova, Svetolk, Dancake. Cover – Dima Zel, Castleski. 4–5 – Artsiom P, dimazel. 6–7 – greenacre8, CC BY 2.0 <https://creativecommons.org/licenses/by/2.0>, via Wikimedia Commons. 8–9 – Scifier, RIA Novosti archive, image #612748 / Alexander Mokletsov / CC-BY-SA 3.0, CC BY-SA 3.0 <https://creativecommons.org/licenses/by-sa/3.0>, via Wikimedia Commons. 10–11 – A.Savin, CC BY-SA 3.0 <https://creativecommons.org/licenses/by-sa/3.0>, via Wikimedia Commons. 12–13 – Memorial Museum of Astronautics, CC BY-SA 3.0 <https://creativecommons.org/licenses/by-sa/3.0>, via Wikimedia Common. 16–17 – Beth Morley. 26–27 – Mil.ru, CC BY 4.0 <https://creativecommons.org/licenses/by/4.0>, via Wikimedia Commons. 28–29 – cla78, Vadim Sadovski. 30 – IM_photo.

Bearport Publishing Company Product Development Team
Publisher: Jen Jenson; Director of Product Development: Spencer Brinker; Managing Editor: Allison Juda; Editor: Cole Nelson; Associate Editor: Naomi Reich; Associate Editor: Tiana Tran; Art Director: Colin O'Dea; Designer: Kim Jones; Designer: Kayla Eggert; Product Development Specialist: Owen Hamlin

Library of Congress Cataloging-in-Publication Data is available at www.loc.gov or upon request from the publisher.

ISBN: 979-8-89232-878-4 (hardcover)
ISBN: 979-8-89232-964-4 (paperback)
ISBN: 979-8-89232-908-8 (ebook)

© 2025 BookLife Publishing
This edition is published by arrangement with BookLife Publishing.

North American adaptations © 2025 Bearport Publishing Company. All rights reserved. No part of this publication may be reproduced in whole or in part, stored in any retrieval system, or transmitted in any form or by any means, electronic, mechanical, photocopying, recording, or otherwise, without written permission from the publisher.

For more information, write to Bearport Publishing, 5357 Penn Avenue South, Minneapolis, MN 55419.

CONTENTS

YOUR JOURNEY TO SPACE

This is **ground control** speaking. We are heading out of this world to follow some amazing pioneers of space.

For thousands of years, going to space seemed impossible. Now, we can send people beyond our world.

Many brave **astronauts** have gone to space. There is so much to discover!

It is time to blast off and start our adventure!

YURI GAGARIN

1934–1968

Our journey begins with a cosmonaut named Yuri Gagarin. A cosmonaut is a Russian space explorer.

In 1961, Yuri became the first person to go into space. He **orbited** Earth in less than two hours.

Yuri's **spacecraft** was designed to break apart on the way back down to Earth. He used a **parachute** to make it to the ground safely.

YURI'S SPACECRAFT AND SUIT

Yuri's journey proved that humans could travel to space.

VALENTINA TERESHKOVA

BORN 1937

Valentina Tereshkova was born in Russia. She spent many hours parachuting from airplanes. This experience earned her a spot in cosmonaut training.

Valentina trained for more than a year before she went into space.

In 1963, Valentina became the first woman ever in space. She traveled in a spacecraft named *Vostok 6.*

Valentina spent almost three days in space. She orbited Earth a total of 48 times.

Valentina had some problems on her journey. She had plenty of food, water, and toothpaste . . . but no toothbrush! Valentina used her finger to brush her teeth.
CCC
Her second problem was much bigger.

Valentina's spacecraft was not set to go back down to Earth. Luckily, she noticed the issue and asked ground control to fix it.

ALEXEI LEONOV

1934–2019

Get ready to step out of the spacecraft! Russian cosmonaut Alexei Leonov was the first person to go on a **spacewalk**.

He wore a special suit so he could breathe outside of the spacecraft.

About 12 minutes into his spacewalk, Alexei noticed a problem with his suit.

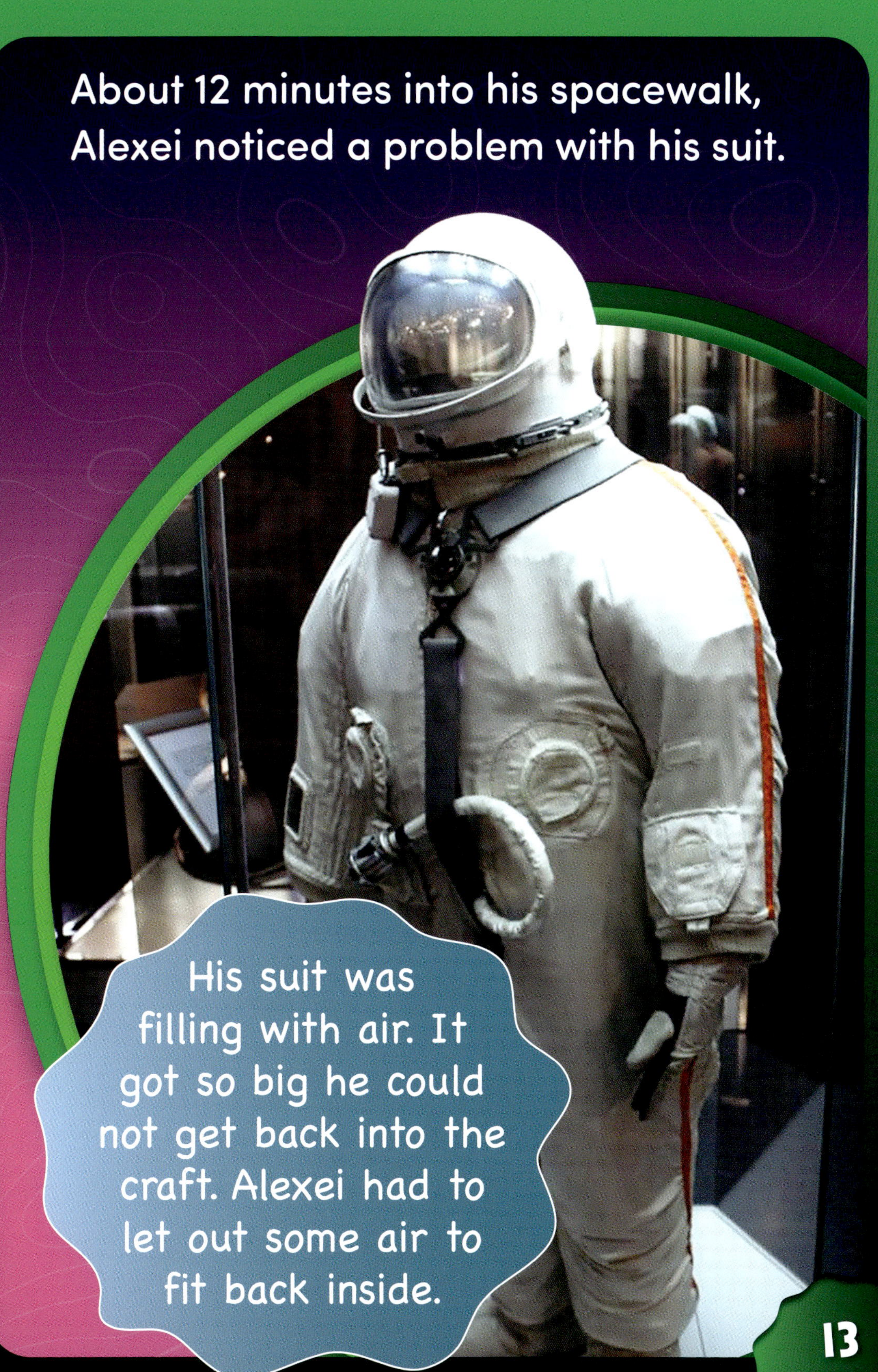

His suit was filling with air. It got so big he could not get back into the craft. Alexei had to let out some air to fit back inside.

NEIL ARMSTRONG AND BUZZ ALDRIN

Neil Armstrong and Buzz Aldrin were American astronauts.

NEIL ARMSTRONG

1930–2012

In 1969, Neil and Buzz were part of the mission to be the first to land on the moon.

BUZZ ALDRIN

BORN 1930

Michael Collins was the third astronaut on the mission. He piloted the main spacecraft.

MICHAEL COLLINS

Once they got near the moon, Neil and Buzz took a smaller craft to the surface. Neil became the first person to step onto the moon. He was soon followed by Buzz.

Millions of people on Earth watched on TV as Neil began walking on the moon.
Then, the astronauts got to work. They spent more than 21 hours on the moon's surface.

While there, they collected rocks and soil. They brought these things back to Earth for scientists to study.

Neil and Buzz will be remembered for doing something that no one had ever done.

GUION BLUFORD

BORN 1942

Our next space explorer is American astronaut Guion Bluford. Before he became an astronaut, Guion was a fighter pilot in the U.S. Air Force.

He was chosen from a group of about 10,000 people to become an astronaut.

In 1983, Guion became the first Black American astronaut in space. He flew above Earth in a spacecraft named *Challenger*.

He helped with many experiments while in space.

Guion was also the first Black astronaut to return to space for a second, third, and fourth mission. He flew back in 1985, 1991, and 1992.

Guion spent more than 688 hours in space.

In 1997, Guion was added to the U.S. Astronaut Hall of Fame.

Guion wants his adventures to **inspire** other Black people to go to space.

KATHRYN SULLIVAN

BORN 1951

American astronaut and scientist Kathryn Sullivan has explored both low and high. As an ocean scientist, she visited the Mariana Trench. This is the deepest known part of the ocean.

As an astronaut, Kathryn went on three different journeys to space.

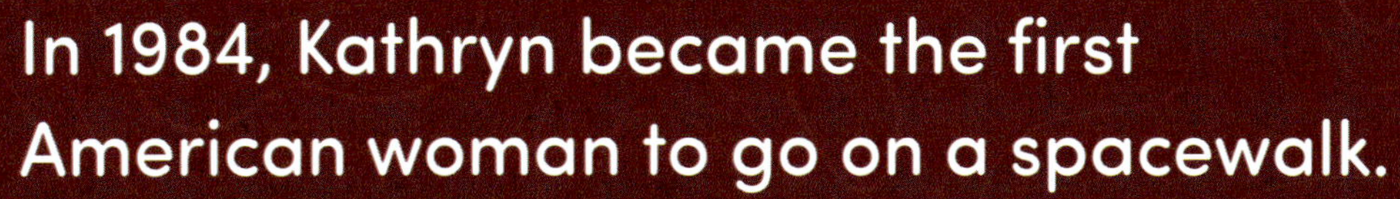
In 1984, Kathryn became the first American woman to go on a spacewalk.

She also helped launch the Hubble Space **Telescope.** The telescope can take pictures of parts of space that are millions of miles away.

HUBBLE SPACE TELESCOPE

SUSAN HELMS

BORN 1958

Our next journey is with American astronaut Susan Helms. She went on five different trips to space.

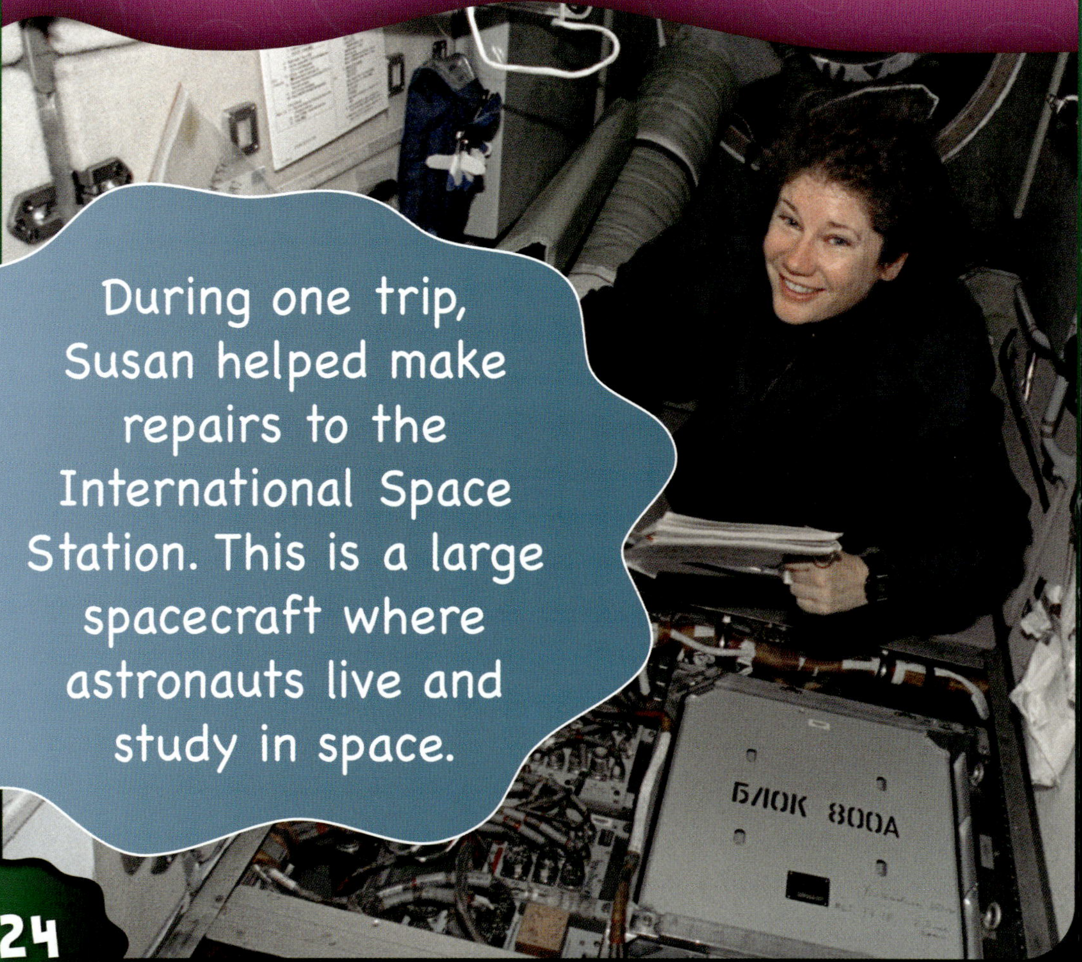

During one trip, Susan helped make repairs to the International Space Station. This is a large spacecraft where astronauts live and study in space.

In 2001, Susan lived in the station. She and another astronaut did a spacewalk that lasted almost nine hours. They broke the record for the longest spacewalk.

Susan is a great explorer. She spent a total of 211 days in space.

VALERI VLADIMIROVICH POLYAKOV

1942–2022

Valeri Vladimirovich Polyakov was a Russian cosmonaut. In 1994, he launched into space for his longest adventure.

Valeri lived in a space station. He studied how space affects the human body.

Valeri spent almost 438 days in space during this one trip.

He orbited Earth more than 7,000 times. Valeri broke the record for the longest stay in space.

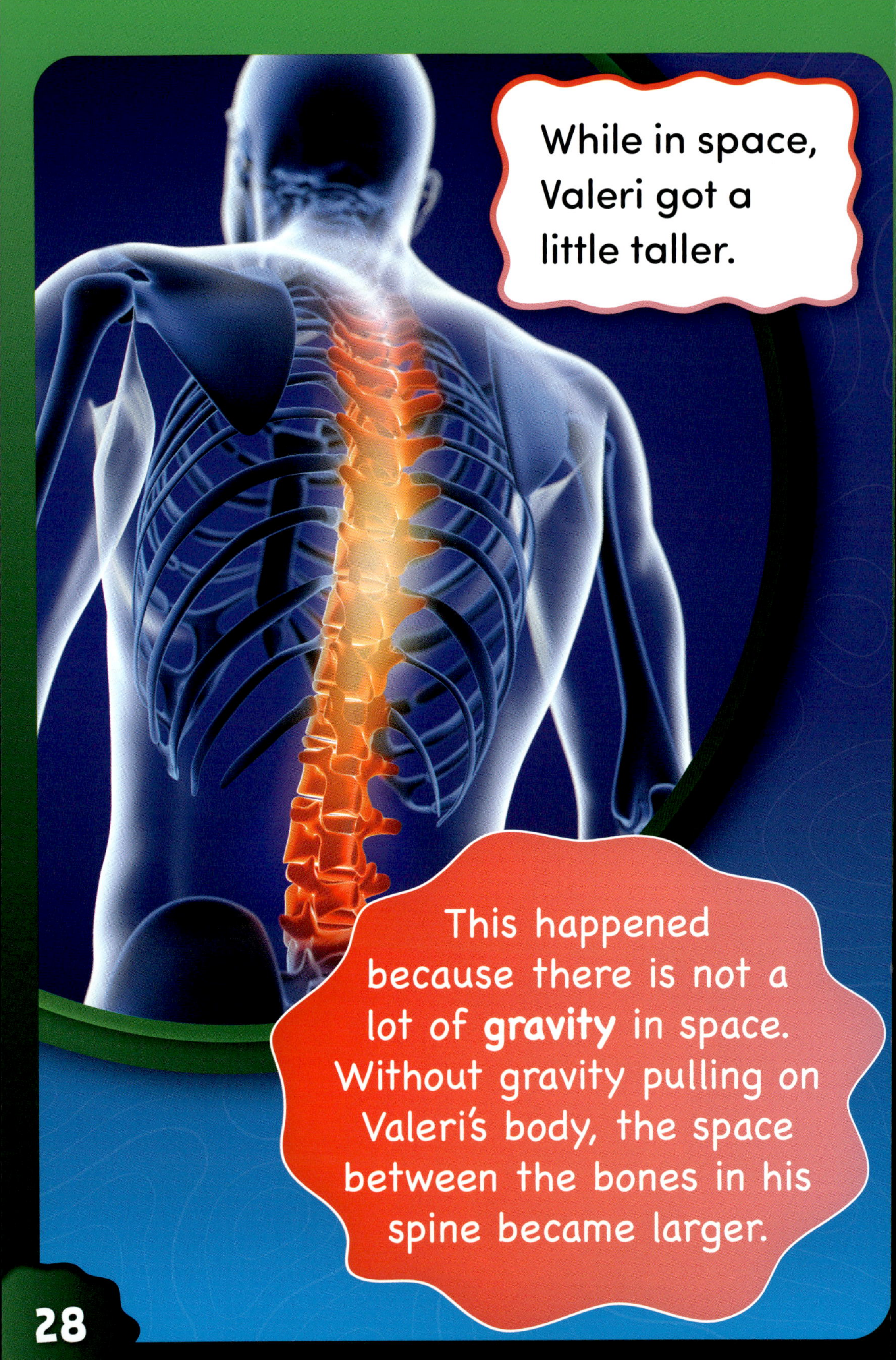

While in space, Valeri got a little taller.

This happened because there is not a lot of **gravity** in space. Without gravity pulling on Valeri's body, the space between the bones in his spine became larger.

Spending a long time in low gravity can be bad for the human body. When Valeri returned to Earth, people were surprised he was able to walk.

Some scientists believe Valeri's adventure shows that people could survive the extra-long journey to Mars.

WHERE WILL A JOURNEY IN SPACE TAKE YOU?

Blasting off to space has been exciting! There is still so much to explore.

Would you like to lead a journey to space? One day, people may talk about your adventures!

GLOSSARY

astronauts people trained to travel to space

gravity the force that pulls things toward Earth, the sun, or other large objects in space

ground control the people on Earth who help with the flight and landing of spacecraft

inspire to motivate someone to do something

orbited moved in a path around another object

parachute a soft cloth attached to ropes that is used to slow down the fall of someone or something

spacecraft a vehicle that can travel in space

spacewalk time spent outside a spacecraft by an astronaut in space

telescope an instrument that uses lenses and mirrors to make distant objects appear larger

INDEX

READ MORE

Morgan, Elizabeth. *Is Exploring Space Important? (Points of View)*. Buffalo, New York: KidHaven Publishing, 2025.

Rains, Dalton. *Future Space Missions (Exploring Space)*. Mendota Heights, MN: Apex Editions, 2024.

LEARN MORE ONLINE

1. Go to **FactSurfer.com** or scan the QR code below.
2. Enter "**Pioneers of Space**" into the search box.
3. Click on the cover of this book to see a list of websites.